RAND M*NALLY

DISCOVERY ATLAS OF PLANETS AND STARS

Rand McNally for Kids™

Books•Maps•Atlases

Discovery Atlas of Planets and Stars

General manager: Russell L. Voisin
Executive editor: Jon M. Leverenz
Editor: Elizabeth Fagan Adelman
Production editor: Laura C. Schmidt
Manufacturing planner: Marianne Abraham

Discovery Atlas of Planets and Stars
Copyright © 1993 by Rand McNally & Company
Published and printed in the United States of America

Library of Congress Cataloging-in-Publication Data

Discovery atlas of planets and stars.
      p.   cm.
   At head of title: Rand McNally.
   Includes index.
   Summary: Maps, illustrations, graphs, diagrams, and
facts provide information on our universe.
   ISBN 0-528-83580-7
   1. Planets--Atlases--Juvenile literature   2. Stars--Atlases--
Juvenile literature.   [1. Planets.   2. Stars.   3. Astronomy.]
I. Rand McNally and Company.   II. Title.   III. Title: Rand
McNally discovery atlas of planets and stars.
QB602.D58   1993
520'.22'3--dc20   93-16805
                                                CIP
                                                AC

Contents

Pluto

Neptune

Uranus

Saturn

The Realm
of the Earth

When placed beside the other planets in our solar system, Earth can be a little hard to find. This portrait shows the solar system's planets and moons, or satellites, at the same scale. The flaming arc at the bottom is all of the Sun that fits into the picture.

A Visit to Our Home Planet

Of the small planets that are closest to the Sun, Earth is the largest. And of all the planets that we know about, Earth is the only planet with life. Life, in all its many forms, is Earth's most important feature. But life on Earth includes many creatures other than humans. According to scientists, people share the Earth with about one million different kinds of animals and more than 350,000 types of plants.

Its surface, a layer of solid rock, is between five and twenty miles (ten and thirty-two kilometers) thick. The Earth's oceans take up about two-thirds of the surface. Humans occupy the highest areas on the planet—the seven continents of Africa, North and South America, Asia, Australia, Europe, and Antarctica.

Unlike any other planet, Earth's surface constantly changes. The surface, or crust, is cracked into a dozen separate plates that move around. Beneath the crust, where temperatures rise above 1,700°F (900°C), rock turns into a thick liquid.

Earth's clouds swirl above Africa (upper left) and mix with Antarctica's ice cap (bottom). Earth is the only place in the universe that we know about where life exists. Our planet is truly a spaceship of life.

Sun

Earth

Length of Year:
365.25 days

Distance from Sun:
92,960,000 miles (149,598,000 kilometers)

Facts About Earth

Diameter:
7,926 miles (12,756 km)

Average Surface Temperature:
58° F (14° C)

Surface Pressure:
1 atmosphere

Atmosphere:
78% nitrogen, 21% oxygen

Length of Day:
23 hours, 56 minutes

Satellites:
1

Satellite Data

Name	Diameter
Moon	2,160 miles (3,476 km)

North
American
Plate

Pacific Plate

In California, two of the Earth's plates are slowly moving past each other. The drawing above shows the two plates. The photograph below shows where the plates meet. This place is called the San Andreas fault.

Under the Earth's crust, liquid—or molten—rock works its way upward in some places. These places sometimes become volcanoes. This volcano is Mount St. Helens in the state of Washington.

A World of Air

A thin shell of gas called the atmosphere surrounds the Earth. If Earth were reduced to the size of an apple, this atmosphere would be as thin as the apple's skin.

Humans live at the bottom of Earth's atmosphere. All of the activity called weather occurs here. Of all the planets in the solar system, only Earth has an atmosphere with the oxygen

Weather has many forms, including several types of storms. The most powerful storm is called a hurricane. This is a photograph taken from above a hurricane. Hurricane winds often reach speeds of over 110 miles (176 kilometers) an hour.

humans need to breathe.

Chunks of rock plunge toward Earth from outer space each day. These rocks, called meteors, usually burn up in the atmosphere. Sometimes, though, they strike the Earth.

The Sun gives off light that we need and light that can harm us. From about ten to thirty miles (fifteen to fifty kilometers) up, a gas called ozone screens out most of the Sun's harmful rays. The place above Earth where ozone exists is called the ozone layer.

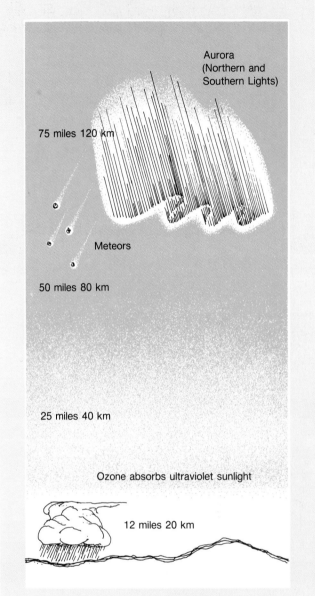

Aurora
(Northern and
Southern Lights)

75 miles 120 km

Meteors

50 miles 80 km

25 miles 40 km

Ozone absorbs ultraviolet sunlight

12 miles 20 km

The Earth's atmosphere protects people from many dangers. Rocks from space as small as dust and as large as automobiles break up in the atmosphere. They sometimes can be seen at night. We call them shooting stars or meteors. At times we can see the aurora, which occurs high in the atmosphere. Storms rage near the bottom of the atmosphere.

Thunderstorms are another type of storm. They are less dangerous to people than hurricanes, but they can be frightening. Here, lightning splits the sky during a thunderstorm in Milwaukee, Wisconsin. Thunder is heard after lightning occurs.

The Moon rises above a cloudy Earth in this photograph. It is Earth's nearest neighbor in space, and the only celestial body on which humans have landed.

The Moon: Our Neighbor in Space

The Moon is Earth's partner in space, its only natural satellite. About 2,160 miles (3,476 kilometers) across, the Moon is an airless, waterless world just one-fourth the size of Earth. It circles the planet once every twenty-seven days at an average distance of about 238,000 miles (384,000 kilometers).

Only one side of the Moon is visible from Earth. The sunlit portion of the Moon's surface—the part seen from Earth—changes daily in a cycle called the Moon's phases.

Marked by ancient basins and giant craters, the Moon's surface has changed very little since it formed. The most important change, at least as far as people are concerned, occurred in 1969. That was when astronauts first set foot on the dusty lunar plains.

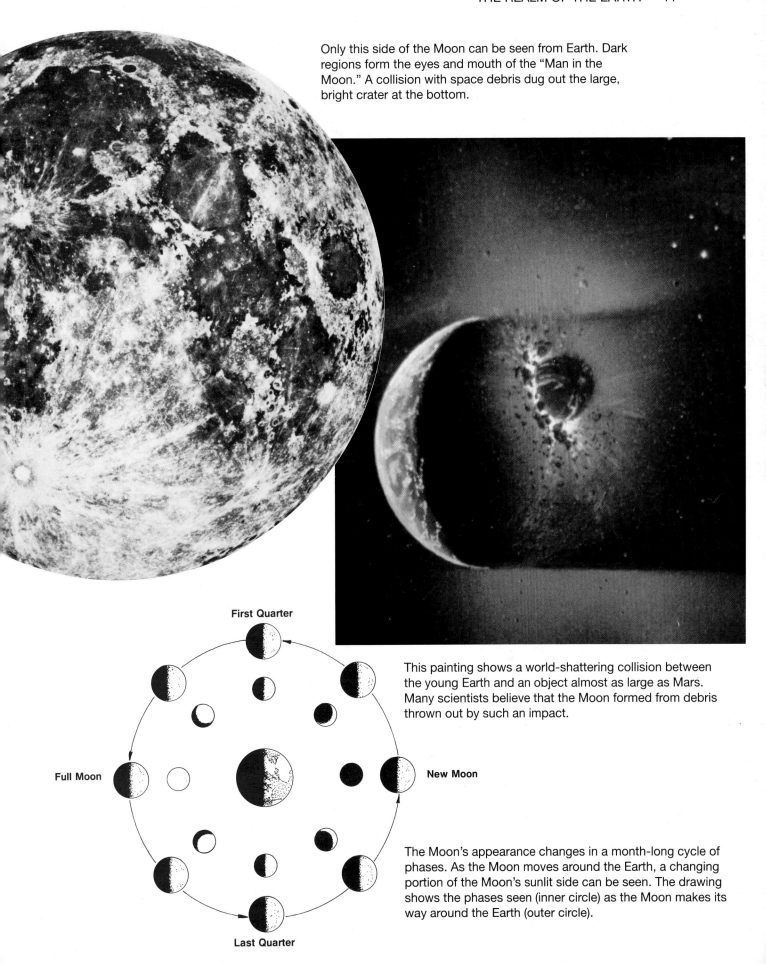

Only this side of the Moon can be seen from Earth. Dark regions form the eyes and mouth of the "Man in the Moon." A collision with space debris dug out the large, bright crater at the bottom.

First Quarter

Full Moon

New Moon

Last Quarter

This painting shows a world-shattering collision between the young Earth and an object almost as large as Mars. Many scientists believe that the Moon formed from debris thrown out by such an impact.

The Moon's appearance changes in a month-long cycle of phases. As the Moon moves around the Earth, a changing portion of the Moon's sunlit side can be seen. The drawing shows the phases seen (inner circle) as the Moon makes its way around the Earth (outer circle).

Venus: A Tortured World

If astronauts headed away from Earth, toward the Sun, they would reach Venus first. Until scientists learned the truth about Venus, the planet was often called Earth's twin. Venus at first seems like a smaller version of Earth. But it is a hot, desert world topped by a layer of acid clouds. The surface is over 850°F (450°C). This temperature is more than twice as hot as a household oven.

Humans have sent many spacecraft to Venus, and they have gathered a lot of information. Some of the spacecraft have actually touched down on Venus, and some of them even sent back pictures. But the surface of Venus is so hot that the spacecraft were destroyed within hours. It seems unlikely that people will be able to land on Venus.

Venus is one of the brightest objects in Earth's sky. Only the Sun and Moon are brighter. Ancient civilizations, especially the Maya people of Mexico, carefully watched the movements of Venus. The planet is never seen all night long. Instead it is in view for only a few hours each night, when it rises before dawn or sets after sundown.

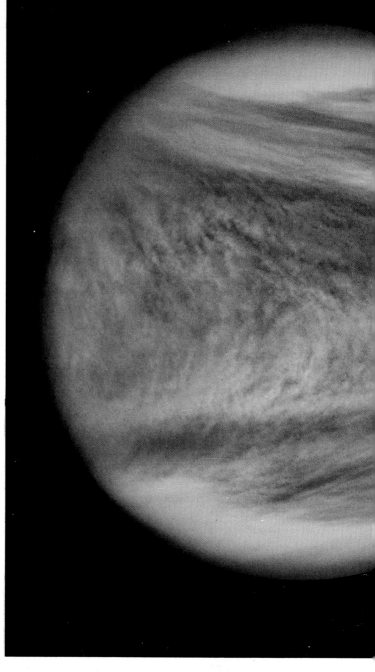

This photograph shows the thick clouds that make Venus one of the brightest objects in the sky. They also hide its surface from easy view.

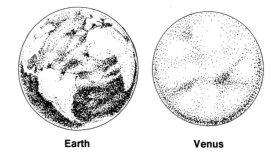

Earth   **Venus**

Earth and Venus, largest of the planets that are close to the Sun, were once thought to be twins. But with a hot, waterless surface and acid clouds, Venus is an astronaut's nightmare.

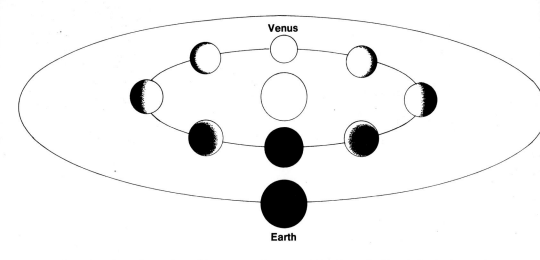

This drawing shows how Venus travels around the Sun. As it travels, it shows its light side or dark side to Earth, just as the Moon does.

Facts About Venus

Diameter:
7,521 miles (12,104 km), or 95% that of Earth

Surface Temperature:
867° F (464° C)

Surface Pressure:
90 times that of Earth's, equivalent to the pressure at a water depth of 3,000 feet (900 meters) on Earth

Atmosphere:
96% carbon dioxide

Length of Day:
243 days, 14 minutes
Planet spins opposite to rotation of Earth

Satellites:
None

This image shows what Venus looks like to radar that can peek through its clouds.

Sun

Venus

Length of Year:
224.7 days

Distance from Sun:
67,241,000 miles (108,209,000 km), or 72% that of Earth

Mars: The Red Planet

The planet Mars is the second-closest planet to Earth. Many ancient civilizations associated its reddish color with the blood of battle and named the planet for their gods of war. Mars is the name of the Roman war god.

Mars continues to fascinate people. It has huge volcanoes, vast canyons, dune fields, and dry channels carved by liquid water. One canyon is so large, it cuts across one-fourth of the whole planet.

On a typical summer day on Mars, temperatures reach no higher than the freezing point, or 32°F (0°C). After sundown, the temperatures drop much lower. The markings on the surface of Mars show that water once ran on the planet, probably when volcanoes melted the ice below the surface. But water would now evaporate on Mars. It is drier than any desert on Earth.

Spacecraft have landed on Mars and searched for life. They have found none. They did find boulder-strewn fields, sand dunes, and a weird pink sky. Scientists are planning more missions to Mars to further examine the Red Planet.

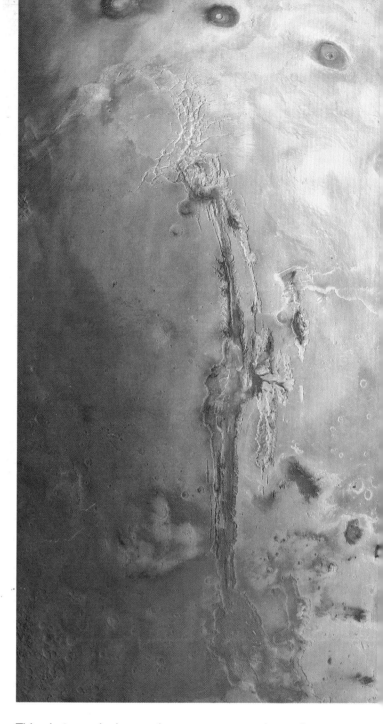

This photograph shows a huge canyon complex and volcanoes. They are far larger than any on Earth. The canyon is about 3,100 miles (5,000 kilometers) long and four miles (seven kilometers) deep in places.

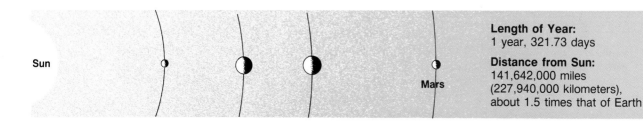

Sun

Mars

Length of Year:
1 year, 321.73 days

Distance from Sun:
141,642,000 miles
(227,940,000 kilometers),
about 1.5 times that of Earth

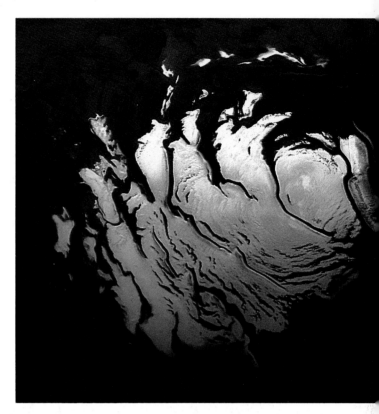

Like Earth, there are ice caps on the north and south poles of Mars. This picture shows the south cap. Unlike the north cap, it contains frozen carbon dioxide, or dry ice, not water.

Facts About Mars

Diameter:
4,222 miles (6,794 km), or 53% that of Earth

Average Surface Temperature:
−13° F (−25° C)

Surface Pressure:
0.7% (1/150th) that of Earth

Atmosphere:
95% carbon dioxide, 2.7% nitrogen

Length of Day:
24 hours, 37 minutes

Satellites:
2

Satellite Data

Name	Size	Discovered
Phobos	17 x 12 miles (28 x 20 km)	1877
Deimos	10 x 7 miles (16 x 12 km)	1877

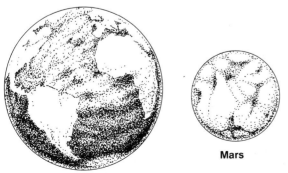

Earth

Mars

The air on Mars is too thin to breathe, the climate is too cold, and there is no liquid water on the surface. Still, it is the most comfortable planet for future human exploration.

Mercury: The Sun-Skimmer

Mercury is closer to the Sun than Venus. It is named for the messenger of the Roman gods. Mercury orbits closer to the Sun than any other planet. From Earth, Mercury is never seen high in the sky or far from the glow of twilight. In fact, it is hard to see Mercury at all.

Like Venus, Mercury shows phases when viewed through a telescope—but little else. Aside from a few vague markings, the landscape of Mercury was a mystery until spacecraft visited the planet. In 1974 and 1975, an American probe made three close approaches to Mercury. It photographed half the planet's surface.

The pictures show that Mercury looks much like the Earth's Moon. It has a heavily cratered surface with plains made during ancient lava floods. Except for new craters carved by meteorites, Mercury's landscape has remained unchanged for eons.

Mercury orbits closest to the Sun. Its landscape is baked by day and frozen by night. This photograph shows Mercury's cratered surface.

Sun

Mercury

Length of Year:
87.97 days

Distance from Sun:
35,985,000 miles (57,909,000 kilometers), or 39% that of Earth

Earth

Mercury

Mercury is about one-third Earth's size.

Facts About Mercury

Diameter:
3,031 miles (4,878 km), or 38% that of Earth

Average Surface Temperature:
340° F, (171° C)

Atmosphere:
Extremely thin, contains helium and hydrogen

Length of Day:
58 days, 15 hours, 30 minutes

Satellites:
None

Like the surface of the Earth's moon, Mercury has many craters. These are formed when meteorites strike the rocky surface.

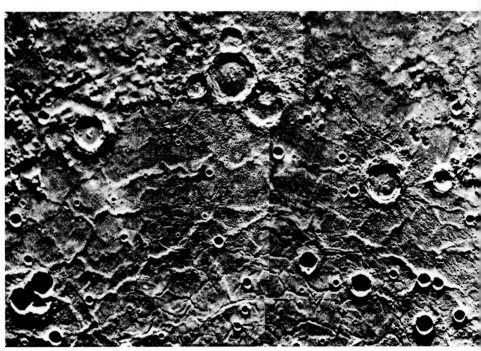

Asteroids and Meteors: Cosmic Debris

Asteroids are rocky objects that circle around the Sun like the planets. But they are far too small to be planets. Astronomers know of some 2,200 asteroids. Most orbit the Sun at distances between 2.2 and 3.2 times farther than Earth, placing them in the gap between Mars and Jupiter. This has come to be called the asteroid belt.

When asteroids run into each other, fragments of rock may break off. These fragments may find their way to Earth's surface. When they streak through the sky, toward Earth, they can be seen as bright fireballs called meteors. When they hit the Earth, they are called meteorites. Meteorites have hit the planets many times. They can form holes, or craters, when they hit.

This painting shows a scene that might have happened. Most scientists think meteorites that hit Earth caused dinosaurs to become extinct.

Facts About Asteroids

Largest Asteroids

Name	Diameter	Discovered	Average Distance from Sun	Length of Year
Ceres	507 miles (917 km)	1801	257,128,000 miles (413,788,000 km)	4 years, 219 days
Pallas	334 miles (537 km)	1802	257,314,000 miles (414,087,000 km)	4 years, 222 days
Vesta	327 miles (526 km)	1897	219,572,000 miles (353,350,000 km)	3 years, 230 days
Juno	167 miles (267 km)	1804	248,018,000 miles (399,127,000 km)	4 years, 131 days

Thousands of years ago, a meteorite created this crater in Arizona. The crater is three-quarters of a mile (1.2 kilometers) across.

About 100 known or suspected craters (black circles) have been identified around the world. Large circles represent the Earth's oldest and largest craters.

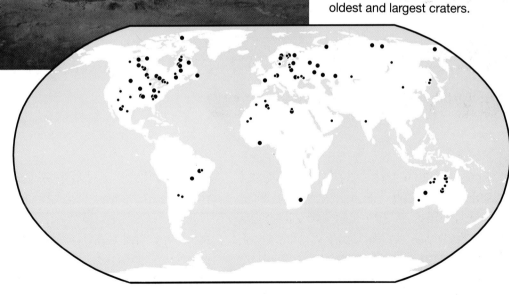

Sun

Asteroid Belt

Distance from Sun: Between 2.2 and 3.2 times that of Earth

Cold and Dark Worlds

This painting shows the planet Neptune from one of its moons. The planets in the outer solar system are very different from the small, rocky worlds that circle close to the Sun. These giant planets are huge balls of gas many times larger than Earth.

Jupiter: King of the Planets

This photograph shows Jupiter and two of its moons, or satellites. The moons, Io and Europa, are both about the same size as Earth's Moon. Io appears in front of the Great Red Spot (left).

Jupiter is the fifth planet out from the Sun. It is by far the solar system's largest world. If all the other bodies in the solar system could be squeezed together, they would make up less than half of Jupiter. To put it another way, the solar system consists of the Sun, Jupiter, and debris.

Jupiter is made of the same material as stars. Like the other giant planets, Jupiter has no solid surface. Storms rage in Jupiter's colorful atmosphere. Lightning is ten thousand times as powerful as what is seen on Earth. All in all, Jupiter is rightly named for the lord of the Roman gods.

Even Jupiter's weather systems make Earth's storms seem small. This is what Earth would look like if it were put next to Jupiter's Great Red Spot, which is a storm system.

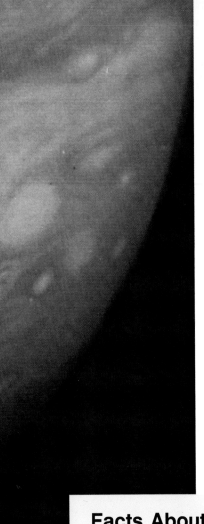

Facts About Jupiter

Diameter:	Temperature at Cloud Tops:	Atmosphere:	Length of Day:	Satellites:
88,700 miles (142,800 km), or 11.3 times Earth's	−234° F (−148° C)	90% hydrogen, 10% helium	9 hours, 56 minutes	16

Largest Satellites

Name	Diameter	Discovered
Europa	1,950 miles (3,138 km)	1610
Io	2,255 miles (3,630 km)	1610
Callisto	2,982 miles (4,800 km)	1610
Ganymede	3,269 miles (5,262 km)	1610

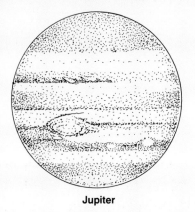

Earth

Jupiter

By any measure, Jupiter is the solar system's giant. To equal Jupiter's bulk would take 318 Earths. Over 1,300 Earth-sized balls could fit within this enormous planet.

Sun

Length of Year:
11 years, 314.96 days

Distance from Sun:
483,631,000 miles (778,292,000 km), or 5.2 times Earth's

Jupiter

Saturn: The Ring Maker

Saturn may be the most beautiful planet in the solar system. It is known for its rings, which are made up of small pieces of ice. Although all the giant planets have rings, Saturn's are the brightest and most complex.

Saturn is second in size only to Jupiter. Like Jupiter and the other giants, Saturn is mostly made of gases. Saturn is more loosely packed than Jupiter. In fact, Saturn is not even as dense as water. If the solar system were a vast ocean, Saturn would float on the surface like a giant buoy.

The bright, icy rings of Saturn show clearly in this photograph. Some of Saturn's moons appear in the foreground. One of them casts a shadow in the light of the Sun onto Saturn behind it.

Facts About Saturn

Diameter:
75,000 miles (120,700 km), or 9.4 times that of Earth

Temperature at Cloud Tops:
–288° F (–178° C)

Atmosphere:
94% hydrogen, 5% helium

Length of Day:
10 hours, 41 minutes

Satellites:
17

Largest Satellites

Name	Diameter	Discovered
Titan	3,200 miles (5,150 km)	1655
Rhea	951 miles (1,530 km)	1672
Iapetus	907 miles (1,460 km)	1671
Dione	696 miles (1,120 km)	1684
Tethys	659 miles (1,060 km)	1684

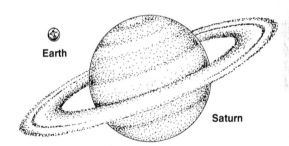

Earth

Saturn

Although Saturn is nearly ten times Earth's size, it contains more liquids and icy substances than rock. Placed in a large enough ocean, Saturn could float.

Scientists used information from *Voyager 2* to create this computer painting of the craft's 1981 flyby of Saturn.

Length of Year:
29 years, 167.25 days

Distance from Sun:
888,210,000 miles (1,429,370,000 km), or 9.6 times that of Earth

Saturn

Uranus: A World on Its Side

Uranus is the name of the Roman god of the sky. This planet is about four times the size of Earth, making it the third-largest gas giant.

Uranus takes about eighty-four years to complete one orbit around the Sun. Unlike the other planets, which spin like tops as they circle the Sun, Uranus seems to be rolling along its orbit. Perhaps long ago an object larger than Earth smashed into Uranus, tipping the planet on its side.

Like Jupiter and Saturn, Uranus is made of gases. It has a ring system, too, and many moons that circle it. The giant planets with their satellites resemble miniature solar systems, with the planets at the center, like the Sun.

Only a few thin, featureless clouds hover over Uranus. Methane gas, which absorbs the reddish colors in sunlight, gives Uranus the blue-green color shown in this photograph.

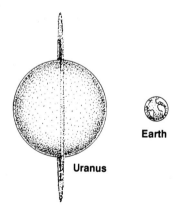

Because Uranus lies on its side, its rings do not appear to circle the middle of the planet like those of Saturn.

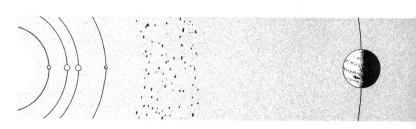

The rings of Uranus were discovered in 1977 when astronomers saw them cut off the light of a star. The particles within the eleven main rings are as black as coal.

Facts About Uranus

Discovered:
1781, by William Herschel

Diameter:
31,700 miles (51,100 km), or four times that of Earth

Temperature at Cloud Tops:
−351° F (−213° C)

Atmosphere:
85% hydrogen, 15% helium

Length of Day:
16 hours, 48 minutes. Planet spins opposite to rotation of Earth.

Satellites:
15

Largest Satellites

Name	Diameter	Discovered
Titania	982 miles (1,580 km)	1787
Oberon	947 miles (1,524 km)	1787
Umbriel	728 miles (1,172 km)	1851
Ariel	720 miles (1,158 km)	1851
Miranda	298 miles (480 km)	1948

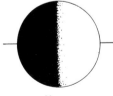

Uranus

Earth

Earth's seasons are caused by the tilt of its axis. The north and south poles each spend about six months tilted into the Sun. But the axis of Uranus is tilted even more. The planet's south pole gets forty-two years of full sunlight; the north pole waits that long for the next dawn.

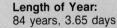

Length of Year:
84 years, 3.65 days

Distance from Sun:
1,786,521,000 miles (2,874,993,000 km) or 19.2 times that of Earth

Uranus

Neptune: The Last Giant

Neptune, farthest of the giant gas planets, lies 2.8 billion miles (4.5 billion kilometers) from the Sun. It takes 165 years to complete an orbit around the Sun. Neptune is slightly smaller than Uranus, but still about four times the size of Earth. Like Uranus, Neptune's bluish color comes from a small amount of methane in the atmosphere.

Like the other giant planets, Neptune has rings. The ring system consists of three thin rings and a broad sheet of dust particles.

The Great Dark Spot of Neptune is a storm system that is as large as Earth. A second, smaller dark spot whirls near Neptune's south polar region. Clouds form a thin, silvery band across the blue planet.

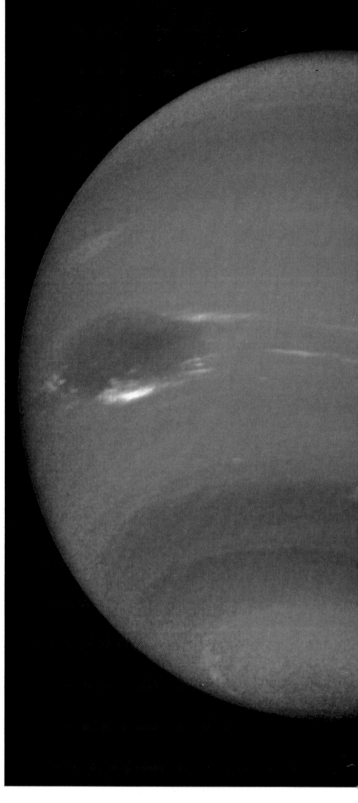

This photograph of Neptune shows the planet's Great Dark Spot. It is a storm system similar to Jupiter's Great Red Spot.

Facts About Neptune

Discovered:
1846, by Johann Galle and
Heinrich d'Arrest

Diameter:
30,200 miles (48,600 km)
or 3.8 times that of Earth

Temperature at Cloud Tops:
–357° F (–216° C)

Atmosphere:
85% hydrogen, 15% helium

Length of Day:
16 hours, 3 minutes

Satellites:
8

Largest Satellites

Name	Diameter	Discovered
Triton	1,690 miles (2,720 km)	1846
1989N1	249 miles (400 km)	1989
Neried	211 miles (340 km)	1949

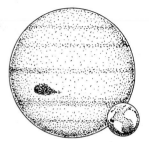

Neptune   Earth

Earth is about one-quarter Neptune's size.

Crystals of frozen gas create bands of white clouds high in Neptune's atmosphere. They cast shadows on the thick blue clouds thirty miles (fifty kilometers) below.

Length of Year:
164 years, 288.54 days

Distance from Sun:
2,798,989,000 miles
(4,504,328,000 km)
or 30.1 times that of Earth

Neptune

An imaginary spacecraft passes Pluto and heads towards its moon, Charon, in this painting. Beyond Charon lies our Sun.

Pluto: At the Edge of Night

Pluto is the smallest, coldest, and most distant planet in the solar system. Discovered in 1930, it remains the only planet found in the twentieth century and the only one never visited by spacecraft from Earth.

Pluto circles the Sun in the strangest path of any planet, taking nearly 250 years to make one complete orbit. From Pluto, the Sun is just the brightest of countless stars in a black sky. Frozen gases like methane and nitrogen form a brittle, icy landscape. Together, Pluto and its moon Charon share the frigid darkness, the farthest worlds known in the solar system.

Pluto Charon

○ ↔ o
11,800 miles (18,880 km)

Earth   **Moon**

○ ◄──► ○
238,000 miles (380,800 km)

Pluto and Earth have one thing in common—their moons are unusually large when compared to the planets themselves.

These images show Pluto and Charon. Like Earth's moon, Pluto's moon is quite large.

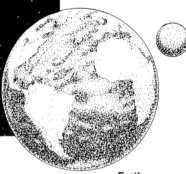

Pluto

Pluto is an icy world only one-fifth the size of Earth. It is the solar system's smallest planet.

Earth

Facts About Pluto

Discovered:
1930, by Clyde Tombaugh

Diameter:
1,416 miles (2,280 km), or 18% that of Earth

Surface Temperature:
–369° F, (–223°C)

Atmosphere:
Extremely thin, contains methane

Length of Day:
6 days, 9 hours, 17 minutes
Planet spins opposite to rotation of Earth

Satellites:
1

Satellite Data

Name	Diameter	Discovered
Charon	721 miles (1,160 km)	1978

Length of Year:
248 years, 182 days
Distance from Sun:
3,666,347,000 miles (5,900,140,000 km),
or 39.4 times that of Earth

Pluto

Comet West, which appeared in 1976, was one of the brightest comets of recent times. Comets have two types of tails, which both show in this photograph. One is a straight, bluish tail of glowing gas and the other is a broad, yellowish fan of dust particles.

Comets: Vagabonds of the Solar System

Comets are the most distant members of the solar system and the least predictable. A bright comet seems to come out of nowhere, its long tail stretching across the night sky for weeks. Then it disappears just as quickly as it heads back into the cold depths of space. Such comets may not be seen again for millions of years, if at all.

Like asteroids, comets are pieces of rubble that remained after the planets were formed. The difference is that comets formed in the outermost fringes of the solar system, far away from the

Famous Comets

Name	Last Seen	Notes
Encke	Always visible through telescopes	Faint comet with shortest orbit known, just 3.3 years to circle sun.
Halley	1986	First comet whose return was predicted (1695, by Edmond Halley); circles Sun every 76 years, due to return in 2061; first comet whose nucleus was studied up close by space probes (1986); observed as early as 240 B.C.
IRAS-Araki-Alcock	1983	First comet named for a satellite (IRAS); passed within 2.8 million miles (4.5 million km) of Earth, second closest comet on record; may never return.
West	1976	Brilliant comet; astronomers watched the nucleus break up as it neared the Sun; not due back for thousands of years.

Comet Ikeya-Seki thrilled astronomers in 1965 by skimming the Sun's surface. It missed the Sun by only 725,000 miles (1.2 million kilometers).

warmth of the Sun.

Astronomers put comets into two groups according to the time they take to circle the Sun. One type completes an orbit in 200 years or less, while the others take longer. The comet with the shortest known orbit circles the Sun in just over three years.

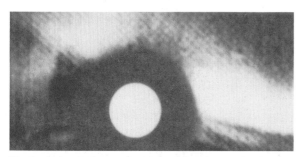

These two photographs show what happened when a comet ran into the Sun in 1979.

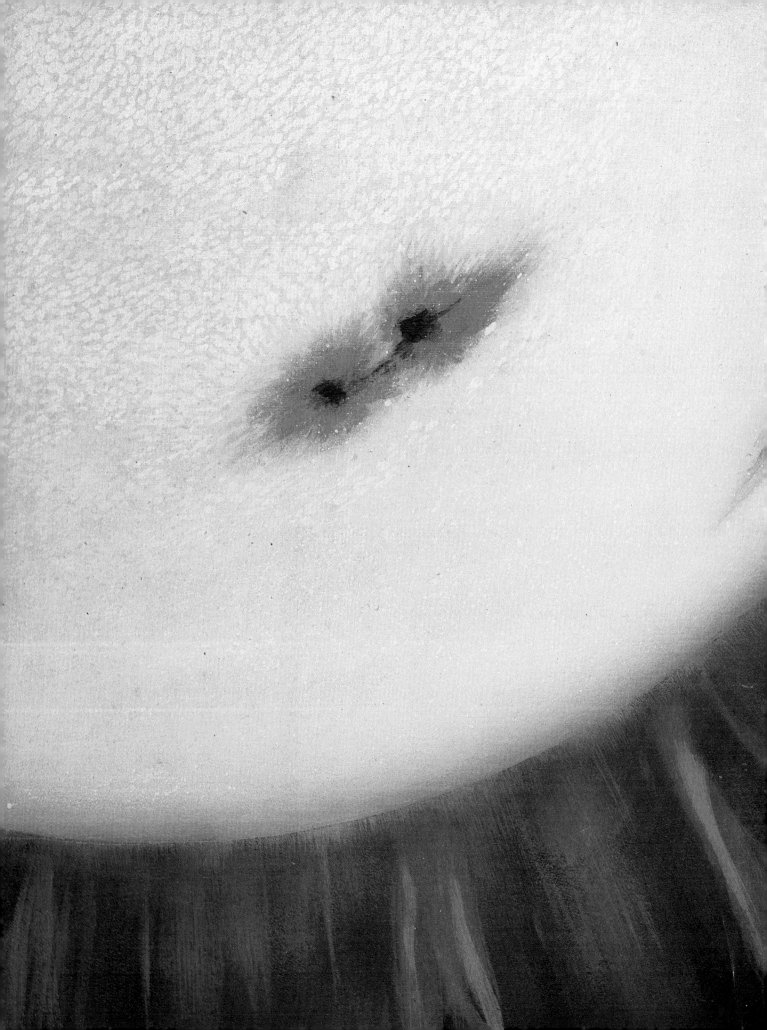

The Stars

The Earth circles a fiery ball of hydrogen and helium gas, a natural nuclear reactor called the Sun. It is also the nearest star. Although astronomers have studied it in detail, its inner workings are still a mystery.

The Sun: The Nearest Star

The Sun is the star around which Earth and the other planets revolve. It is the largest body in the solar system, some 750 times bigger than everything else put together. It is Earth's source of light and heat. It is, quite simply, the nearest star.

The Sun is a huge ball of hydrogen and helium gas some 865,000 miles (1.4 million kilometers) across, or nearly 110 times Earth's size. On its surface, the temperature is 11,000°F (6,000°C). The gases heat up at deeper levels, until the temperature reaches 27 million°F (15 million°C) deep within the Sun's core.

Actually, all the planets lie within the outermost part of the Sun. There is a thin stream of particles that flows out from the Sun and fills the space between the planets. It is called the solar wind. The solar wind pushes back the glowing gases of a comet to create the comet's tail.

The Sun's hot outer atmosphere is called the corona. It stretches millions of miles above the Sun's surface. During a total solar eclipse, the corona appears as a glow around the darkened Sun.

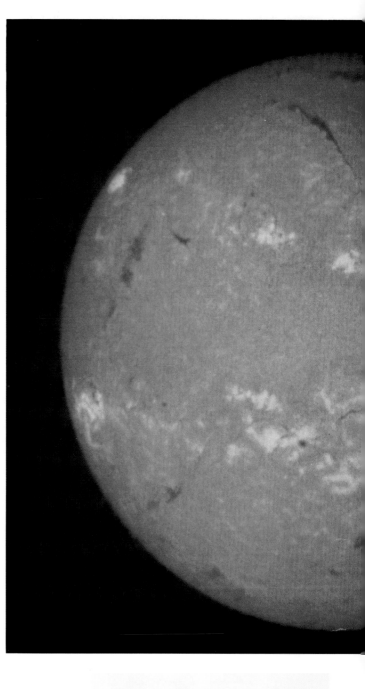

Facts About the Sun

Diameter:
865,000 miles (1,392,000 km), or 109 times that of Earth

Mass:
333,000 times that of Earth

Surface Temperature:
10,300° F (5,700° C)

Central Temperature:
27 million° F (15 million° C)

Composition:
70% hydrogen, 27% helium

Spin (at equator):
26 days, 21 hours

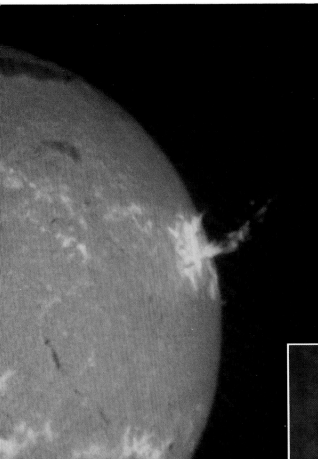

This photograph of the Sun shows a jet of gas blasting thousands of miles into space. This event occurred in June 1989 and is one of the largest on record.

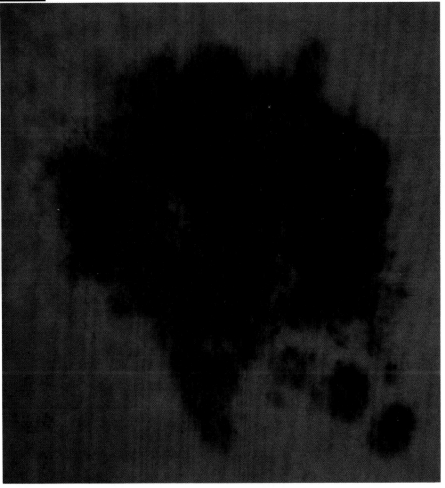

Sunspots are pockets of cooler gas on the Sun's surface. This group, which appeared in March 1989, is many times larger than Earth.

The Great Nuclear Reactor

The Sun is a natural nuclear reactor. The energy and heat the Sun gives off affect the entire solar system. Astronomers believe the Sun to be an average-sized, middle-aged star. At its current energy output, the Sun's fuel will last another five billion years.

Sunspots are dark patches on the Sun's surface. They are pockets of cooler gas sometimes half the temperature of surrounding regions. Sunspots can cause outbursts called flares. The energy released in one hour by a large flare could power a major city for 200 million years. Flares can also damage satellites, interrupt radio and TV signals, and create beautiful lights called the aurora.

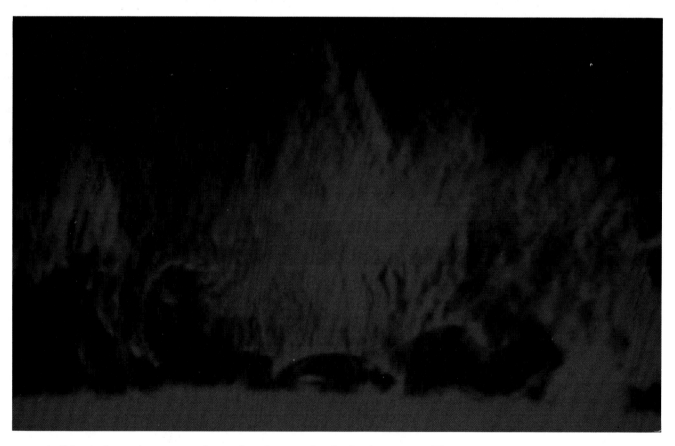

In this photograph, a mass of gas rises thousands of miles into space. These huge arcs can be seen stretching into space along the edge of the Sun.

A total eclipse of the Sun occurs when the Moon passes between Earth and the Sun. For a few minutes, the Moon blocks the bright ball of the Sun and the surrounding glow, or corona, can be seen.

A solar eclipse occurs when the Moon passes between the Earth and Sun. In a lunar eclipse, the Earth is between the Moon and the Sun. Eclipses can be full, like the photograph above, or partial, when only part of the Sun or Moon is in shadow.

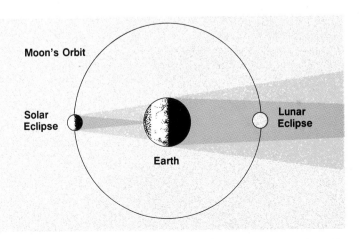

Moon's Orbit

Sun

Solar
Eclipse

Earth

Lunar
Eclipse

A Star Is Born

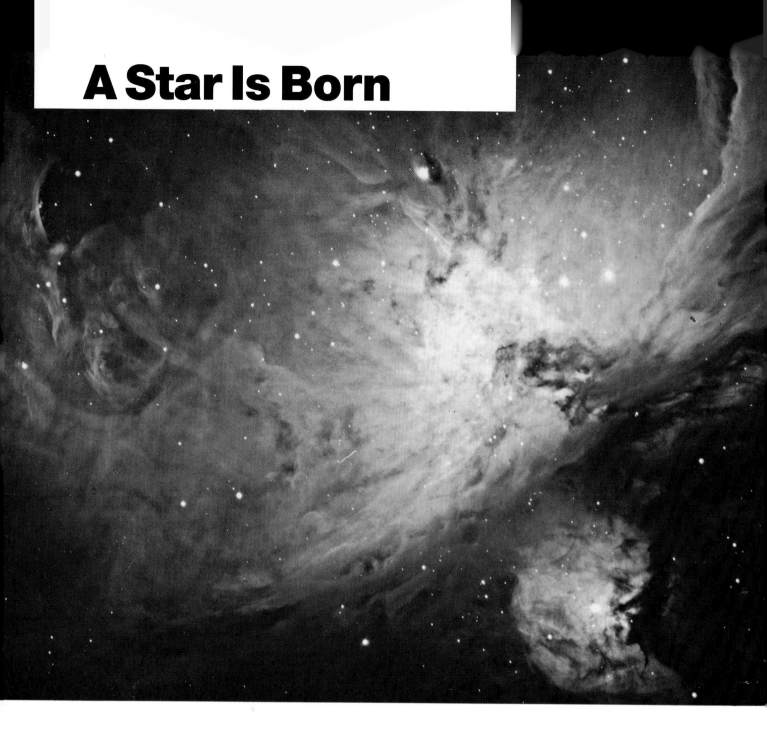

About five billion years ago, the Sun began its life deep within the darkness of a giant cloud of gas and dust, or nebula. Part of the cloud became compressed. More gas and dust joined this cloud, and soon gravity pulled it even closer together. This loose ball of gas and dust kept contracting, heating up as it shrank and spinning ever faster. Deep within the cloud, temperatures and densities soared to a critical point. The star's furnace was lit, and the cloud became our Sun.

The outer portions of the cloud that formed the Sun were flat. Dust particles collided, stuck together, and collided

Glowing with the light of newborn stars, the Great Nebula in Orion is a place where many stars are born. Behind this glowing veil lies the dark cloud where star birth occurs.

Star-forming regions in the constellation Orion show up as red areas in this map made by a heat-sensitive telescope. The white dots show the location of bright stars.

again to make the building blocks of the planets. When the Sun lit its internal fires, flares and a violent wind swept much of the gas out of the inner solar system. Rocky bodies formed near the Sun, and the planets that were giant balls of gas formed farther out.

The Sun has brightened somewhat since its early days. Its rotation has slowed, its flares have settled down, and its activity follows a steady eleven-year cycle. Not much will change for the next five billion years.

A Red Giant

Every star wages a battle with gravity. Gravity tries to compress the star still further, but the the star's core creates a balancing pressure. In about five billion years, the Sun will begin to lose its battle.

The Sun's crisis will begin when the fuel in its core begins to run out. Over a period of two billion years, the Sun's fires will die down. Gravity will pull inward, and the Sun will grow smaller and hotter. It will begin using fuel outside of its core. Now at a higher temperature, the Sun will expand a little.

This process will continue until the Sun has expanded to 100 times its present size. The Sun will fill the Earth's sky. Earth's surface, as hot as 2,600°F (1,430°C), will be a sea of liquid rock. The Sun will become a red giant.

The Sun's red giant stage will last 250 million years. Another energy crisis will then force it to contract and heat up.

The photograph of a star shows a cloud of dust around the star. The painting shows what the cloud may look like close up.

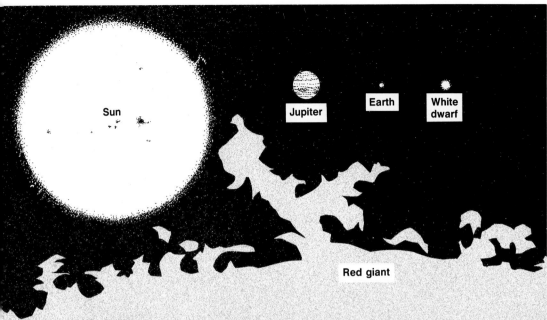

The Sun's life began when it formed over 4.5 billion years ago. In another five billion years, it will redden and swell to 100 times its present size. This drawing shows relative sizes.

This painting shows the progression of the Sun throughout its life. Its size changes as it ages, first ballooning to a red giant, then shrinking to a planet-sized white dwarf.

This photograph shows the wreckage of an exploded star. It is called the Crab Nebula, and it contains a neutron star. Because this neutron star emits pulses of light and radio waves, it is called a pulsar.

A White Dwarf

Pueblo Indian carvings in Arizona caves may record the sudden appearance of a supernova near the crescent moon on the morning of July 5, 1054.

Eventually the Sun will settle into a new routine. The energy from the core will slowly blow off the outer layers of its atmosphere until the core itself is revealed. What is left of the Sun will be crammed into a hot, Earth-sized ball. The Sun will become a white dwarf.

As a white dwarf, the Sun's light will be a thousand times weaker than it is today. At the age of fifteen billion years, the Sun will slowly cool and fade for several billion years. Then the planets will circle a black, burned-out cinder.

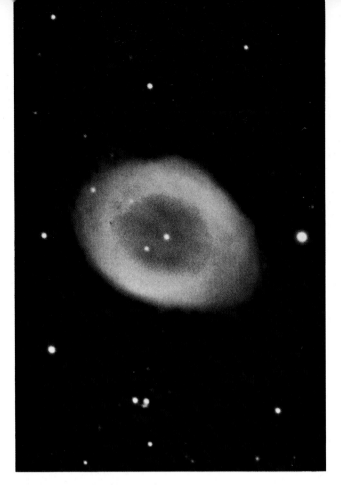

Some twenty thousand years ago, a star blew off its outer layers and created this expanding shell of gas.

In 1941, the violent explosion of a supernova (marked with the line) lets one star briefly outshine all the others in the galaxy.

There are worse ways for a star to go. Those much larger than the Sun experience a far more violent end. These stars end up in an explosion that blasts the star apart. This explosion is called a supernova. A supernova may leave behind a small, dense object called a neutron star or even a black hole, from which light cannot escape.

Although as many as three supernovas may occur in Earth's galaxy each century, none has been seen for more than three hundred years. No one knows when the next one will appear, but the Milky Way is overdue. In 1987, a supernova exploded in a small nearby galaxy. The star briefly became as bright as some of the brightest in the sky. As the shell of gas from the star blew away, the supernova faded from view.

The Galaxy and Beyond

A galaxy is a system of stars, planets, and other objects. This is what the Milky Way, the Earth's galaxy, might look like from far out in space.

The Milky Way

This photograph shows the thickest part of the Milky Way. The center of the galaxy lies about 28,000 light-years in this direction.

Our Earth is part of our solar system, and our solar system is part of our galaxy. We call our galaxy the Milky Way, because it appears to us as a softly glowing band that winds its way along the night sky. It is the combined light of billions of stars so far away they cannot be seen individually. It is our view, from the inside out, of our own galaxy.

The glow of the Milky Way forms a band because the galaxy is flattened into a disk. The glow is brighter in one direction because in that direction lies the very center of the galaxy. Stars are not all the galaxy contains. There are also great clouds of gas and dust that are the factories where new stars are created.

The scale of the galaxy is far beyond that of the solar system. Miles or kilometers may work for stating the distances to planets, but they are much

Facts About the Milky Way Galaxy

Diameter:	Mass:	Distance between spiral arms:	Thickness of galactic disk:	Satellite galaxies:
100,000 light-years	About 200 billion suns	6,500 light-years	1,300 light-years	2 (visible only in the southern sky)

Satellite Data

Name	Mass	Diameter	Distance
Large Magellanic Cloud	10 billion suns	40,000 light-years	173,000 light-years
Small Magellanic Cloud	1 billion suns	30,000 light-years	225,000 light-years

The brightly glowing gas of the Lagoon Nebula, about 3,300 light-years away, marks it as a site where stars are being born.

too small to deal with the vast distances within the Milky Way. Instead, astronomers use a measurement based on the speed of light. Light travels through space at a speed of 186,000 miles (300,000 kilometers) per second. In one year, light tracks 5.88 trillion miles (9.5 trillion kilometers). This distance is called the light-year. The Milky Way is about 100,000 light-years across and 1,300 light-years thick.

A Spiral Galaxy

The top photograph shows a group of young stars about 10,000 light-years away. The bottom photograph shows a globular cluster about 16,000 light-years away. The cluster contains perhaps a million stars.

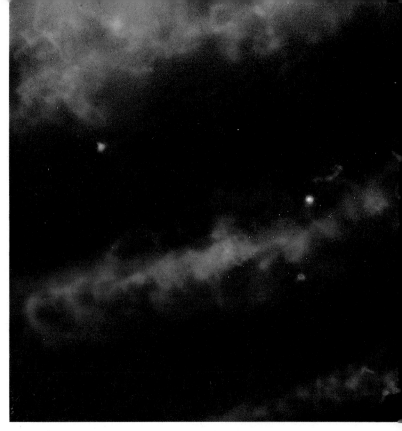

This painting shows what three of the spiral arms of the Milky Way might look like from above. The Sun is within the arm in the center.

The Milky Way is roughly a ball of older, redder stars set within a flat disk of gas, dust, and younger, bluer stars. The galaxy revolves, and it has arms that spiral out from the ball in the center. Our solar system lies within one of the arms of the Milky Way. It takes about 200 million years for our solar system to orbit once around the galaxy.

On the outside of the Milky Way, there are great balls of stars. They are called globular clusters, and they, too, orbit the center of the galaxy.

Still farther out are two small, odd galaxies that also travel around the Milky Way. They are called the Magellanic Clouds, named after the explorer Ferdinand Magellan, whose crew discovered them in the early 1500s.

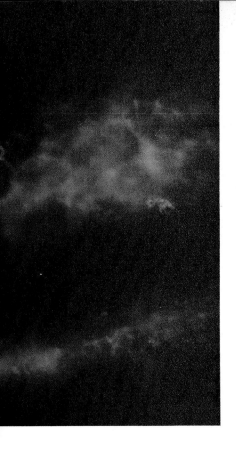

These two paintings show the Milky Way from the top and from the side. Our galaxy is a typical spiral galaxy about 100,000 light-years across and 1,300 light-years thick. Several globular clusters orbit the inner galaxy.

Galactic Neighbors

It is difficult for humans to imagine the size of the universe. Shown in this photograph is one of our closest galactic neighbors, the Andromeda Galaxy. It is 2.2 million light-years away. This distance is close in terms of the size of the universe.

Most large galaxies are spirals like the Milky Way. Their bulging central regions are filled with older, redder stars. Hot, young stars create the uncoiling spiral arms.

Although spiral galaxies rotate, the arms of the spiral do not rotate in one piece. Their inner parts circle the galaxy faster than their ends. The arms stretch and break away. Before this occurs, however, new stars begin forming in the arms to preserve the spiral pattern.

A hundred years ago, many scientists thought that the Milky Way was all there was in the universe. They were not sure what all the other unexplained objects they saw in the sky were. It is only in the last few decades that humans are able to look into the night sky and know that some of the glowing bodies they see are stars, and some are whole galaxies.

This is one of the Magellanic clouds, a neighbor of the Milky Way. It is a large, unorganized collection of stars and gas that orbits our galaxy.

The gigantic galaxy shown in this photograph contains some three trillion stars, enough to make dozens of Milky Way galaxies. The small fuzzy "stars" are actually some of the ten thousand globular clusters of stars that orbit it.

The Milky Way is part of a group of galaxies called the Local Group. The Andromeda Galaxy is also in the Local Group, and it is one of our closest galactic neighbors. It is about 2.2 million light-years away. The Local Group surrounds us to distances of about 3.3 million light-years. In terms of the entire universe, stars and galaxies in the Local Group are truly our close neighbors.

Andromeda
Galaxy

Leo II
Leo I

Ursa Major
Sextans

Ursa Minor
Draco

Milky Way

LMC
SMC

Pegasus   Sculptor

Fornax

This drawing shows the nearby galactic neighborhood, called the Local Group. The circles mark intervals of one million light-years. The Milky Way and Andromeda spirals are the group's two largest masses.

More on Galaxies

The Milky Way is a called a spiral galaxy because of its shape. There are other types of galaxies with other shapes. Another type of galaxy, for example, looks very different from the colorful spirals. It is round and made up of billions of stars. These galaxies range in size from tiny dwarf galaxies with only a few million stars to vast masses of trillions of stars. Other galaxies are disorganized collections of gas, dust, and stars.

The gravity of galaxies holds them together. Within three million light-years of the Milky Way there lie about two dozen galaxies of all shapes and sizes. This cluster of galaxies is called the Local Group.

This loose spiral holds only about 10 percent of the Milky Way's mass. A member of the Local Group, it lies some 2.6 million light-years away.

Partly hidden by a band of dust, this giant galaxy contains perhaps 300 billion stars.

This photograph shows a classic spiral galaxy. Arms rich in gas, dust, and newborn stars uncoil from its center.

The Distant Universe

The Local Group, the small cluster of galaxies that includes the Milky Way, is small and loosely packed. Beyond it there are other clusters of galaxies. The distances between galaxies and galactic clusters make our Earth and solar system appear very tiny and insignificant in the vast space of the universe.

Galaxies cluster together because they interact with one another's gravity. The Milky Way and the Andromeda galaxy, for example, orbit about their common center of gravity within the Local Group. Smaller galaxies move around the larger ones. The Local Supercluster is an assembly of galaxy clusters that includes the Local Group. Gravity holds clusters together, but superclusters must slowly spread in different directions. Still, they are the largest structures scientists know of, stretching up to 300 million light-years across.

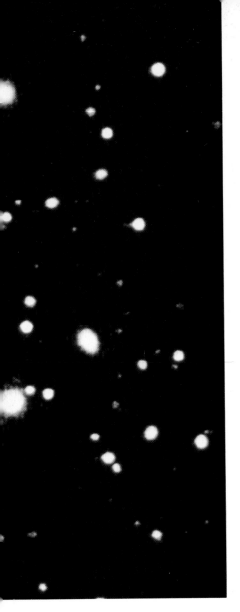

This photograph of the distant universe shows not only stars but also galaxies. The two large yellow lights are enormous galaxies some 500 million light-years away.

Quasars are possibly galaxies like the Milky Way in the first stages of formation. In this painting, the galaxy's spiral arms are almost lost in the glare of its brilliant, exploding core.

The farthest objects astronomers have found in the universe are quasars. They look like stars, but they let off far more energy than hundreds of giant galaxies put together. The incredible amount of energy they release makes them visible across billions of light-years. No one knows what fuels these mysterious objects.

First discovered in 1963, over six hundred quasars are now known. The farthest quasars are more than ten billion light-years away. They were shining even as our own galaxy was taking shape, and so quasars represent a glimpse of the distant past. Quasars may be the bright cores of young galaxies undergoing a violent stage of formation.

The View from Earth

The glow of the Milky Way highlights this midsummer star party. The constellation of Scorpius the Scorpion rides high above the horizon. The Milky Way is the combined light of billions of stars too far away to see.

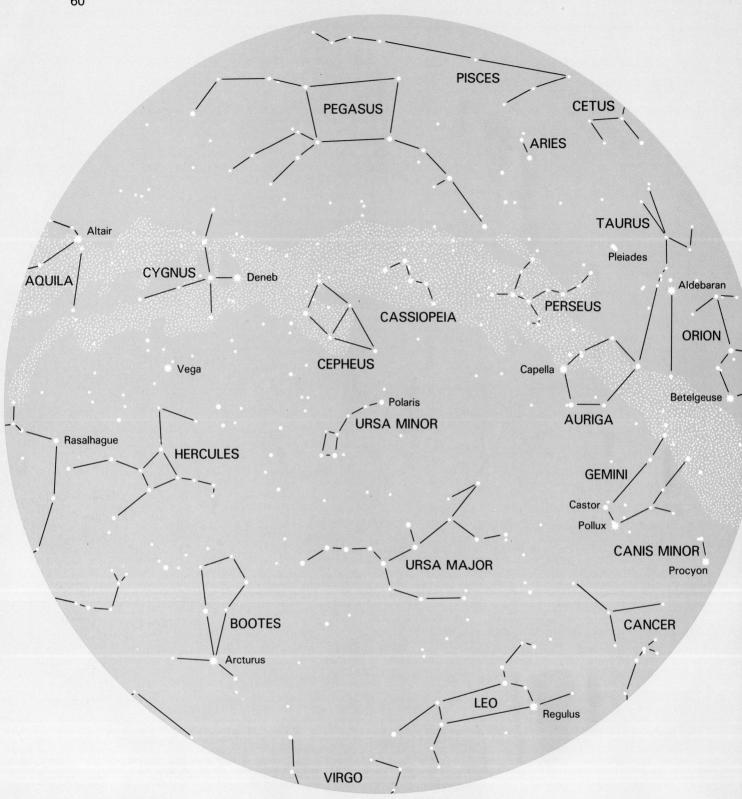

The Northern Sky

These star charts show the brightest stars in the northern and southern skies. Each chart shows how the night sky would look if seen from the Earth's North or South poles. The gleaming band of the Milky Way snakes all around and reaches its brightest in the southern sky. Two small galaxies, the Magellanic

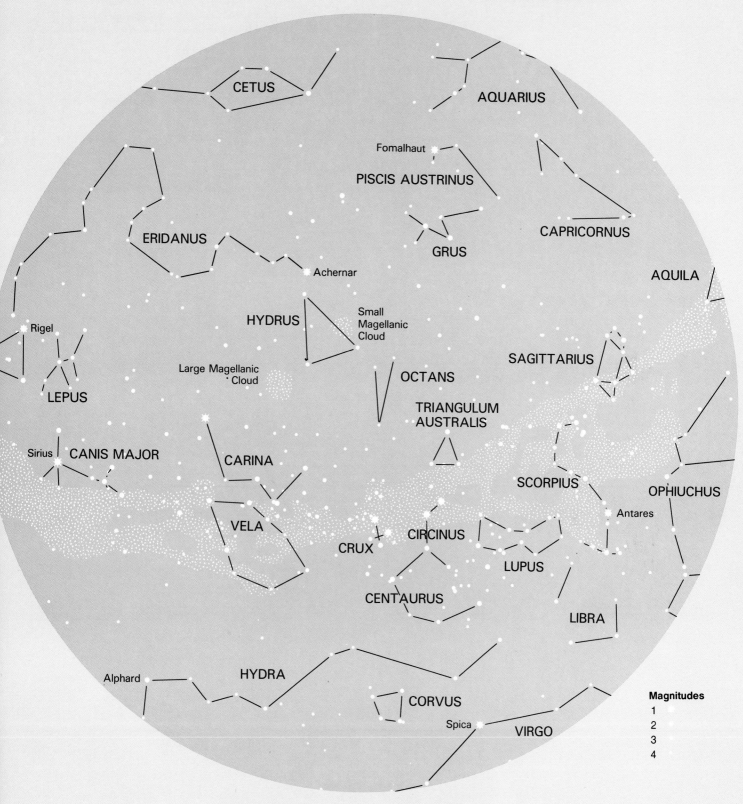

CETUS

AQUARIUS

Fomalhaut

PISCIS AUSTRINUS

ERIDANUS

GRUS

CAPRICORNUS

Achernar

AQUILA

Small
Magellanic
Cloud

HYDRUS

Rigel

SAGITTARIUS

Large Magellanic
Cloud

OCTANS

LEPUS

TRIANGULUM
AUSTRALIS

CANIS MAJOR

Sirius

SCORPIUS

OPHIUCHUS

CARINA

Antares

VELA

CIRCINUS

LUPUS

CRUX

CENTAURUS

LIBRA

HYDRA

Alphard

Magnitudes
1
2
3
4

CORVUS

Spica

VIRGO

The Southern Sky

Clouds, appear in the southern sky. Companions of
our Milky Way Galaxy, these small star clouds can be
seen well only from south of the equator.

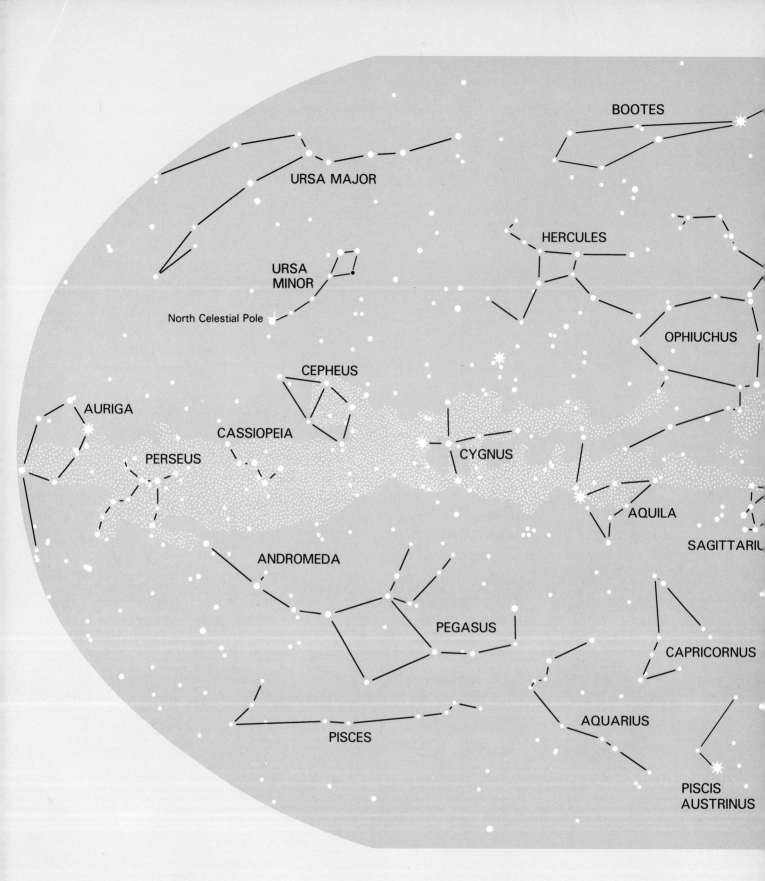

BOOTES

URSA MAJOR

HERCULES

URSA
MINOR

OPHIUCHUS

North Celestial Pole

CEPHEUS

AURIGA

CASSIOPEIA

CYGNUS

PERSEUS

AQUILA

ANDROMEDA

SAGITTARIU

PEGASUS

CAPRICORNUS

AQUARIUS

PISCES

PISCIS
AUSTRINUS

The Galaxy
from Within

Piecing together the Milky Way is a difficult task.
We see it only from a small planet, and only from the
inside. This drawing reveals the galaxy as it would
appear if we could see it from the outside. The north

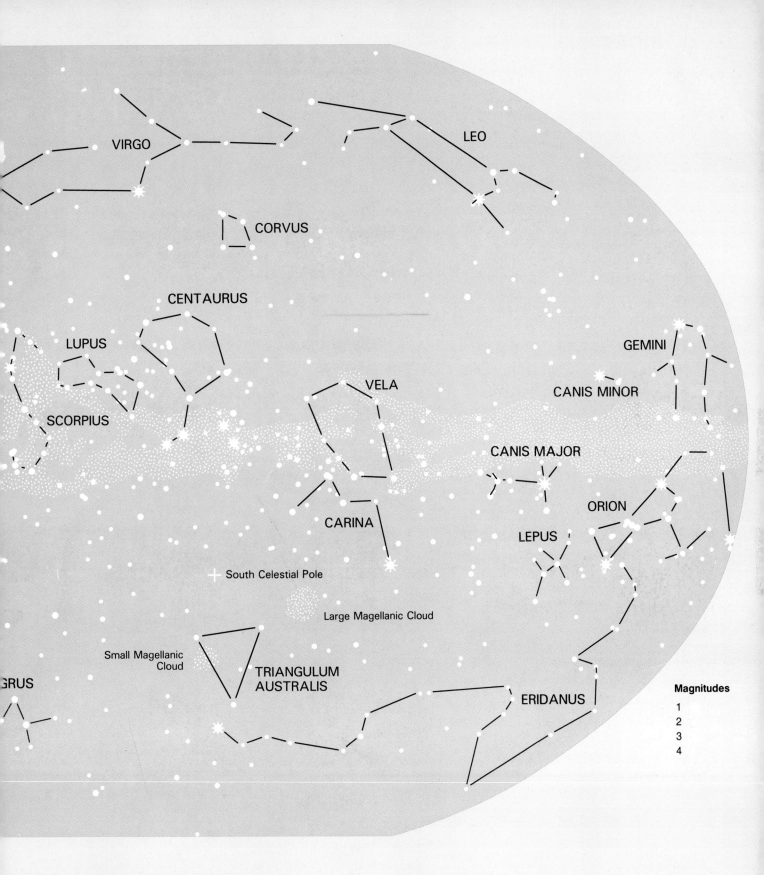

VIRGO

LEO

CORVUS

CENTAURUS

LUPUS

GEMINI

CANIS MINOR

VELA

SCORPIUS

CANIS MAJOR

CARINA

ORION

LEPUS

+ South Celestial Pole

Large Magellanic Cloud

Small Magellanic Cloud

TRIANGULUM AUSTRALIS

GRUS

ERIDANUS

Magnitudes
1
2
3
4

(left) and south (right) celestial poles, the points around which the night sky seems to rotate, are marked by crosses. The Milky Way runs through the center. The

number of bright stars dwindles far north or south of this line. The Milky Way's satellite galaxies, the Magellanic Clouds, appear at lower right.

Index